DRC RICHEST AND POOREST COUNTRY

DRC RICHEST AND POOREST COUNTRY

James Kazongo

To order additional copies of this book, contact:
Xlibris
1-888-795-4274
www.Xlibris.com
Orders@Xlibris.com
738083

CONTENTS

Introduction xi

How To Build an Honest and Great Country 12

DRC Land Of Blessing 15

The Untouchables 18

Self-affliction 24

Fiscal Indiscipline 26

Embezzlement 27

How to Cure Economic Ailment in DRC 33

Tourism Development 39

How to Engage Into Beneficial
Negotiation with Chinese 41

Political War or Economic War 44

Democratizing DRC 53

ADDECO (Alliance Des Democrates Pour le
Developpement Economique du Congo) 61

To my kids, Michael, Matthew, and Maxim, you guys are my pride and joy. The fact of staying away for two years from you guys was the most difficult time in my entire life. Daddy will always love you.

To my wife, Jeanine, thank you from the bottom of my heart for your prayer and support. I dearly love you.

To all the G20, despite our differences and argumentation that we went through days and night for two years of incarceration in Pretoria, South Africa, I love you all.

Pastor David Bakajika, Etienne Tara-tibu Kabila, Patrick Masikini, Jeff Kilele, Chadrack Kilele, Olivier Omari, Petit Nelka Tenda, Tshibangu Musa, Papa Jean Pierre Kayembe, Jean P. Moura, Mobuto Eric, Petit Paty Kakiese, Jacob Mapima, Maitre Joe Ngesi, Alain Yoka, Apolinaire Mayele, Commandant Felly Simon Mokuna, and John Malako, you are Congolese heroes, and you will always be remembered in history of DRC.

Betty James, you are the definition of friendship. Thank you for your support, you will always be on my mind.

Brother Placide, I will be damn if I forget you. All the fun we had during the trial, and all the sacrifices you did for us by risking your job, thank you very much.

To Pastor Joseph, Pastor Jules, Pastor Isaiah, Pastor Chris, Father Bongi, thank you for your prayers and support.

To all the compatriots Congolese who supported us during the ordeal, Emmanuel Ilunga, Papa Boketshu, General Ngando, Brother Benjamin, and all of you that I forgot, may God Almighty bless you and the Democratic Republic of Congo.

INTRODUCTION

DRC has a population of 75 million. The most populous Francophone country, it seats by the Congo River basin, covers nearly 390,000 square miles. The country outlets to the Atlantic Ocean, has narrow land in the north bank of the Congo river. It's located in Central Africa, bordered by nine land boundaries, Angola, Burundi, Congo, Uganda, Rwanda, South Sudan, Tanzania, Zambia, CAR, DRC is the second largest country in Africa after Algeria—considering that Algeria has a large part of its desert in its territory. DRC lies on the equator line. Its climate is hot and humid in the river basin, and cool and dry in the Southern Highlands.

Cold Alpine climate in the Rwenzori range, sometimes it's called the mountain of the moon. Located on the border between Uganda and the DRC, the Rwenzori Mountains reach heights up to 16,761 feet. The peaks of its mountains are permanently snow capped, the principal rivers are the Ubangi, Bomu in the North, Kasai and Congo River in the west. The Lake Tanganyika lies entirely along the eastern border with Tanzania and Burundi. DRC has a tropical climate. Hot and humid near the equatorial river basin, cooler and dry in the South and East, north of the equator has rain season that starts from April to October, and dry season from December to February, south of the equator rainy season starts from December to February, south of the equator rain season starts from November to March and dry season starts from April to October. The average temperature during the rainy season is 65F to 95F.

It has vast terrain in the Central Plateau covered by tropical rainforest. Surrounded by mountains in the west, plains and savannah in the south and west, and grassland in the north. The country's rainforest contain great biodiversity including the Chimpanzee and the Bonobo. Five of the country's national parks are listed as world heritage sites: the Garamba, Kahuzi, Biega, Salonga, and Virunga national parks; and the Okapi wildlife reserve. The civil war and government mismanagement and poor economic. Conditions have endangered much of this biodiversity. Many park rangers were either killed or could not afford to continue their work. DRC has so many natural resources such as cobalt, copper, cadmium, petroleum, diamond, gold, silver, manganese, tin, germanium, uranium, radium, bauxite, iron ore, coal, hydropower, timber, coltan, etc.

The Congo River and its basin is the second reservoir of fresh water in the world after the Amazon in Brazil. It is important to mention the numerous huge fishing lakes around the oriental borders as well as inside the country.

Long ago, before MySpace, Facebook, Twitter, and Instagram, Ian Douglas Smith (then Prime Minister of Rhodesia, now Zimbabwe) had staggering briefing by Rhodesian security council, and was about how the USSR now Russia was setting methodically in Northern Africa and kept moving on the new territory once the previous territory had been secured, they might have had a pretty good shortstop who relentless kept stealing bases. Their goal was to monopolize Africa in terms of resources and minerals. DRC was one of the countries the communists have been longing for.

Unfortunately, back then there was something called capitalism and communism. Each and every one of them had to play hard to protect its own house. The United States of America preempt Russia after being alerted to this development, and as a result, the American Congress Committee on Strategic Minerals and Mining sent an envoy to DRC and a couple of Southern African countries, precisely Zambia and Zimbabwe. After that visit, they came up with very compelling reports, in the most expressive language

termed "The Persian Gulf of Strategic Minerals of our Planet."
All the list of strategic minerals were itemized. Thanks to
Americans, Russia struck out and could not gain control of
DRC, the "Warehouse of Strategic Minerals of our plane," if
I may rephrase it.

The United Nations recently, in 2012, had assessment
on DRC outlining the potential that DRC has to become
a global economic powerhouse. The key finding of that
study conducted in conjunction with DRC environment
ministry are:

- the DRC has the highest level of biodiversity in Africa
- the DRC's tropical rainforest extends over 1.55
  million square km, and accounts for more than half of
  Africa's forest resources, making them a critical global
  economic system provider and potential close to $1
  billion in annual revenue.
- It's untapped mineral reserves are estimated $24
  trillion.
- The Congo River basin supports Africa's largest inland
  fisheries with an estimated production potential more
  than 600 tonnes per year.
- The DRC represents the jewel in the Persian Gulf of
  Strategic Materials

A very interesting point is the study was conducted by the
United Nations in conjunction with DRC's environmental
ministry in 2012 underlining the potential of Democratic
Republic of Congo to become a global economic powerhouse.
Why this study only taken place in 2012? Is the DRC historical

events? Why it took the UN and Congolese Government so long to conduct that study only in 2012 to determine that potential? DRC was discovered and was colonized under Belgium for eighty years, so the potentiality always have been there.

The Democratic Republic of Congo has a tremendous diversity of minerals, diamonds, gold, cobalt, copper, uranium, cotton, and tantalum just to name a few, and I still strongly believe that DRC has a mineral that is yet to be found and named. That particular mineral will have a miraculous impact on mankind the way electricity is being generated, our communication system or the way the data is being saved. I could not meticulously explain it, but let alone future determine. Besides all these minerals, DRC has 50 percent of Africa's forest, which includes 80 million hectares of Arable land. A great opportunity for agriculture, as I did indicate earlier, the Congo River basin has the potential to produce 600 tonnes per year of inland fisheries. Inga River can conceivably provide hydroelectricity to the whole Southern African countries at the very least. While we are living in the age of electronic devices such as laptops, iPhones, cell phones, Xbox, iPad, DS, tablet, etc., all these devices use rechargeable batteries, which is made from cobalt in their electrode. In 2011 DRC produced 48 percent of cobalt in global requirements.

Almost everyone in the world owns a part of DRC if they have a laptop or a cell phone, which is made from coltan. The Democratic Republic of Congo is one of the leading producers for that mineral called coltan. While the DRC is a rich country in terms of resources and yet so poor in terms of life standards, but from laptops to cell phones, cars to airplanes, and all kinds of everyday items are made using minerals that come from the DRC, I would not be exaggerating if I openly declared that the world depends on the DRC. The repetitive and constant demand for portable electronic devices has created a huge market for minerals. In 2010, DRC mining exports valued at an estimated $9 billion, nearly half coming out from cobalt, while ironically, the country is rated at the bottom of the wealth chart of its air transport industry. It is pumping up resources used by other countries to make airplanes. Jet engines use superalloys that often contain cobalt, chromium, and aluminum alloys, while DRC is supplying the world with its resources.

The life standard of Congolese people is very deplorable. It is rated as the poorest country in the world, and the revenue per capita is very dire. The majority of Congolese live with less than $1.00 a day. DRC is full of resources and should not be impoverished country. Now, what are the steps that need to be taken to tackle this predicament? It's not just a simple arithmetic, there is a lot of X's and Y's involved. First, we have to take a close look at the root cause of most of Congo democratic problems. It prematurely gains its independence from Belgium in 1960. DRC former leaders with few years of education were mistakenly convinced that they could get behind the wheel of this latest model vehicle and zoom it without any manuals or help. Unfortunately, this vehicle had a gas tank, breaks, and most of all, it needs service every 3,000 miles. The colonists needed extra time to show how to operate and maintenance. Impatient they were, they did not have the time for advice. Not having the notion that the car needs gas, and the run this vehicle to the ground and completely totaled.

When Belgium punched out its time card, there was nothing prepared for the next day. No manufacturing industry to transform our raw materials. We were still entirely dependent on colonists. For instance, our gold will be sent to Europe, so they can make a bracelet out of it and ship it back to DRC, so it's something like this. A gram of gold costs, for instance, $10.00, they purchased 2 grams for $20.00 to make a bracelet. The same bracelet, they turned around and sold it for $60.00 and their profit, $40 out of this business. That is a very smart business, the one that comes on late night TV telling you how to use somebody else's money and become rich. I bet DRC's leaders never seen that late night commercial.

Infrastructure roads and bridges were and still part of country's problem. When Belgium's shift was over, Kinshasa had two major roads in 1960—there were not any interstate roads so to speak. Most roads in Kinshasa or large cities like Lubumbashi, Mbandaka, Kisangani, Kananga, Bukanu, Mbuji Mayi, Bandundu, Matadi were not asphalt, and DRC's leaders failed miserably to even asphalt or create new roads. Not having the slightest of knowledge that roads and bridges are our major factor to enhance the economy of the country, the next chapter will explain in integrality. DRC's economic problem cannot be addressed without resolving its politics.

Most analysis would quickly point out a bloody civil war that took more than 9 million lives of Congolese and colonial oppression, as the reasons for its economic debacle. I would much rather not go that route because that war was intentionally orchestrated in order to destabilize the country. The main source of this economic Armageddon is the homegrown dictatorship, corruption, regionalism, and tribalism. Nepotism dictatorship has been the leading cause of DRC's problems. Democratic Republic of Congo has a handful of those dictators and tyrants so far. From Mobutu to Kabila, DRC leaders lack a sense of leadership; they lack ability to inspire, motivate, and are careless about the welfare of their people once their offshore accounts are healthy. They are ready to sacrifice their own people for their own personal interests. They are not receptive to the ideas of their subordinates, they deprived them from telling the truth and speaking their own minds, and the outspoken ones always end up in prison. They institutionalized tradition in their constitution. Once president of DRC, by the way of coup d'etat, assassination, or bogus election, the country automatically became their private property. They have the power to kill, destroy, uproot, steal, and sell without congress' or parliament approval.

Let's look at certain illegal business that took place during the administration of Joseph Kabila. Congolese President sold a mining enterprise owned by Gecamines to an Israeli businessman for $15 million a few months after. The smart Israeli businessman are sold the same mining to a London listed Kazakh mining firm from $75 million so for $15 Million that Mr. Dan Gertler, best friend of Joseph Kabila spent, Mr. Gertler profits $60 million. Kabila sacrificed Congolese people for only $15 million for his personal account. I would call it high treason. It seems like one friend is smart, and the other one is a sucker and stupid. Kofi Annan, a former

UN secretary general, looked at five deals struck by 2010 and 2012 by Joseph Kabila and compared the sums for which government owned mines were sold with independent assessments of their value. He found a gap of $1.36 billion, double the state's annual budget for health and education. These deals were just a small subset of all the bargains struck according to Kofi Annan. It seems like Kabila's best friend is the negotiator and deal maker for Kabila on Congo's minerals and mining. Last year, London listed Kazakh mining firm paid a $1.25 billion settlement to first quantum, a Canadian Minerals Co. After being stripped by Kabila and severed ties with Mr. Gertler for $550 million, the IMF cancelled its loan program with Congo after Joseph Kabila refused to explain all these deals between Gecamines, the state-owned miner; and Mr. Gertler. Joseph Kabila would much rather impoverish Congolese people than expose his best friend— the CEO and Chairman of Congo Minerals and Mining for their personal accounts.

Congo's resources are scandalously uncontrollable and mismanaged and mostly in the hands of foreign companies and corrupt leaders. Last year, miners in Congo which Freeport-McMoran and Glencore Xstrata shipped $6.7 billion worth of copper and cobalt from the country. It would be far more if the country was better governed. To hang on to power, the dictator Kabila has been dishing out Congo resources to some of the African tyrants and dictators to help him sustain his power. South Africa has been the ringleader for helping the dictatorship regime of Mr. Joseph Kabila. Former South African president Mbeki T made millions and millions of dollars from Congo's resources, the actual president polygamist Jacob Zuma and his nephew owned several mines in Kalanga along with his son. In return, South Africa would send its soldiers to protect Joseph Kabila's regime, the only president in the world that all the Presidential guards are foreign.

One of the things he does is together with Jacob Zuma of South Africa. They will create war in Eastern Congo to destabilize the Congolese Army, a truck load of minerals start leaving DRC territory to South Africa via Rwanda. That is one of the reasons Rwanda became a producer of coltan and gold in the world because everything comes through Rwanda and ship either by air or road to South Africa. Also with the blessing of Joseph Kabila, Rwanda would create M23 (a Rwandan rebels) to do the same procedure—I mean created a bogus war.. I'm afraid the Eastern Congo War will never end unless there's a responsible government in Kinshasa. There is also a multitude of small foreign mining corporations that have for partners Congolese ministers and governors, and totally leaves Congolese people out and behind, so those foreign companies and Congolese officials are the worst nightmare for Congolese people.

Then, with millions of dollars, Congolese presidents and officials steal from Congolese. They open bank accounts in Switzerland and buy houses in Paris, Brussels, South Africa, and even Florida. I wonder why western presidents and officials once elected, they don't go to DRC and purchase houses. DRC leaders are still mentally colonized? Or are they suffering inferiority complex? Or just flat out idiots? Because most of their Swiss bank accounts and chateau automatically become unclaimed property after their death, or thrown out by the next team of tyrants unless they died in a plane crash with $16 million dollars in cash. So maybe their relatives would be able to retrieve a couple hundreds, which I doubt, because if a poor Congolese reached that wreckage of that plane first, it becomes a free money bowl.

Another way to rip Congolese people, most Congolese officials created unimaginable number of ghost employees and divert their salaries to their pockets. The banking system is ineffective. Most of Congolese officials and businessmen keep a ton loaded of money in their houses. Since DRC is preposterously governed, it'll give money to any foreign country to come settle and make their own law, wild central, If I may say so. That is why you'll see in Kinshasa Pakistani and Lebanese have their own police and military to mistreat Congolese. Some do have private prisons. These Pakistani and Lebanese are supported by members of army forces and Government to oppress Congolese.

Another reason for Congo's problem is corruption. If you think cracking rock is hard, try fighting corruption in Congo. Now, why the Democratic Republic of Congo is one of the countries that corruption is daily bread? Because there is a humongous gap between haves and have nots. Police stop cars for no reason, force their way in, and refuse to leave until paid off. They will do the same to pedestrians to show them identification. If you do have your ID, they will go further to ask you for baptism card or check your shoes if the heel is crooked that is an infraction, they will tell you to pay a fine for that because they are agents to put orders. Tax agents will harass businessmen until you have paid them off. Police and tax agents do this crime to survive. They are not paid regular and their salaries run between \$40–\$50 a month (at the same time, the president's making about \$500,000 a month.)

I met Oliver, a tax agent from Kinshasa who has not been paid for eight months, explain to me that he gets paid \$50 a month. Sometimes, it lapsed five months without getting paid. When they finally decide to pay them, they are corrupt because of insufficient pay or no pay at all for months, while the top officials of those institutions are making truck loads of cash—that's where the corruption revolution keeps on coming. Now let's look at the key important people in society. Teachers, Congolese teachers make about \$50 periodically a month. So that alone would put them in no mood to do their job properly.

Corruption is spread in all national levels. It became a second or part time job for the employees to compensate for their insufficient pay or no pay. Shortcoming, you can't get anything accomplished in DRC unless you're prepared mentally to pave your way with corruption when you're being approached by a policeman for identification in DRC, clearly it means he's asking you for money. Birth certificate means money, business license means money, there is time you need to corrupt just so you can breathe. Now in the whole dynamic all this, better yet in scheme of thing if you don't have money in DRC. Just forget about how this world works. Just keep on breathing until you die.

Corruption only became prevalent in DRC after independence. I believe it could have possibly existed during colonial times, but in small scale of things. Unlike western countries, a (symbiotic) corrupt relationship only existed between the state and mega companies in which those companies helped the state to stabilize development, while the state offered heavy subsidies and protection to those companies. DRC corruption is an epidemic that corrupts both private and public sectors due to this self-centered interested behavior. The country is left in state of no progress, and that prevents it from moving forward and improving the lives of its citizens.

HOW TO BUILD AN HONEST
AND GREAT COUNTRY

How can we create a truly great country? Of course, service delivery, health, education, the economic, and many other areas of government, but at the heart of success of all those areas of national striving are great leaders with consciousness. The habits and no having predisposition have played a major role in sustaining much of the existing culture of corruption. It's apparent expansion is also the ramification of a culture deeply entrenched in DRC. It is very terrifying to comprehend, having legally empowered bodies to oversee the public and private sectors will probably be the first step of fight corruption in DRC. But that alone would not work because all these institutions will quickly be corrupted. As I was saying, we need great leaders with consciousness. That also will not be changed subsequently. Above and beyond that, the responsible government needs to renew people's minds by implementing sanctions and penalties to the violators through judicial system punishment. Churches can work in conjunction with the state for renewing people's mind by preaching sounds gospel, and demonstrating that corruption is a sin. That only will reduce corruption by 30 percent the first five years in DRC. Not only is that an essential key to promote human dignity, and honestly, all this will inspire and create the moral and ethical values in society. And this will eradicate credence, selfishness, and self-enrichment at all times.

In order to have a moral society, DRC people need to overcome corruption whether driven by personal gain, dishonesty, favoritism, nepotism, or other motivations. We have to have for motto to serve not to steal. It is a well known fact that a country where corruption overshadow will fail it's endeavor to create a just and prosperous dispensation for its people. Corruption is not only bad for DRC government and reputation of it's people, it is also detrimental to the growth of the economy, job creation, and the overall development of DRC. Due to present irresponsible government and lack of civic education, a majority of Congolese have yet to cross the bridge of tribalism and regionalism. They are still reflecting on that diverse culture and committed to those ideals and unethical values that divide them from each other. They failed to recognize or to overcome tribalism and regionalism on the basis of culture and tradition instead of striving for national unity.

Tribalism and regionalism also prevent equal opportunity employer, prevent competent and fair management and employment practices that always result in broad base racial, and gender representation, which gives way to favoritism that lack scrutinizing candidates for compatibility and experiences and ends up placing unqualified applicant just for because the employer and employee are from the same region or tribe. That also created a pool of highly qualified jobless people in DRC.

Unlike Nigeria, South Africa, Sudan, and some other African countries where tribalism and regionalism are main causes for war, xenophobia, hatred, and enmity, DRC tribalism has never initiated any animosity between its people (except favoritism). Mobutu government deserves a lot of credit for that. Though he was a vicious dictator, he was in same time unifier and advocate for the National Unity, and that gave birth to make inter tribal marriage. You will also see a native of equator region will be happy to live and work in Kasai region, bas Zaire to Haut-Zaire and vice-versa. When Mobutu was toppled by other tyrants and dictators Laurent Kabila all this national unity went down the drain. Kabila was more of a tribalist than an uni during his administration. All the public institutions was dominated by people who speaks Swahili, armed forces officials, police officials, any members of government institutions were filled with Swahili. Their situation tried to raise some concern up till now, but luckily, Congolese are still holding it together. To use tribalism and regionalism as one of the components for DRC government, mismanagement, and poverty will be unfair. Those elements only have impact in employment levels, not in social, political, or economic level. Congolese have peaceful coexistence and mutual respects for each other. Their past never was hostile and prejudice, and their future could only be better with responsible leaders.

DRC LAND OF BLESSING

America might and still be the land of opportunity, but DRC is the land of blessing. There is no ambiguity. The United States of America will give opportunity to any human being regardless of their gender, belief, sexual orientation, color, gay, and straight. To work hard in order to succeed any venture they may well envisage. In this formula of success, the key word is work hard. DRC is quite opposite. The odds of becoming a millionaire in DRC is greater than anywhere else in the world if you only have a small startup capital. Most Europeans become billionaires just by stopping in DRC for a visit. Senegalese made millions of dollars for years. They will come and settle, open a corner store with a couple of cigarette packs and samousa on their shelves as bogus business, and real objectivity is the exploitation of minerals advance. Taking advantage of DRC's incompetent government to suck out billions of dollars from DRC. The saddest part is, none of these people even have a bank account in DRC. All the money that they swindle always send back to their original countries for its development, while DRC people are still being on the bottom of the rock economically, and their capital revenue is two times less than the World Bank's standard benchmark of poverty.

DRC has been cheated billions of dollars every year without government knowledge, and that has done a tremendous debt to DRC's economy. Chinese are coming. They are everywhere in the remote corners of DRC, sucking up its minerals illegally. Who knows what's next? Could be Talibans, Al Qaeda, or Isis till they will end up being bombed by United States Special Forces. Would you blame all these foreigners for taking advantage of DRC's irresponsible government? DRC needs to review its immigration system and foreign economy law. If only it exists. Also review its border policy, and implement a strong supervision on its border, so minerals and billions of dollars don't swiftly move in and out. Its borders are revolving doors. Foreign companies are also to blame, but I would not put that blame entirely on them. How do they get there in the first place? That is the ultimate question. Let's start with a brief explanation concerning law and regulation for exploitation of minerals substance in DRC.

The mining sector in DRC is managed and regulated by the Mining Ministry Department under section called Mining Code and Rules. "Cadastre Minier" is a branch of mining ministry department that deals strictly and responsibility with the registration of any applicant who's applying for mining business in DRC. This department provides all the applications that needs to be filled in order for a foreign firm or an individual entrepreneur to be licensed and allowed to do mining business. After all applications have been filed and processed by the government through the Mining Ministry department, then it will specify what category of minerals to be exploited (gold, diamond, cobalt, copper, coltan, etc.). The "Cadastre Minier" then will issue a mining research permit after government approval of the application the mining firm, or entrepreneur will start doing the research. After his satisfaction, the Department of Mining Division will then transfer the license from mining research permit to exploitation permit, and the firm will be established in the region's capital. In conjunction and association with civil society, *confession religieuse*, and all different tribe chiefs of each province. The law exists, but as usual, DRC doesn't play with the rules—bad governing of DRC (Anti valeurs). As corruption, frauds, fiscal evasion, fiscal incivic in this domain make it very difficult for the country and its citizens to benefit from its mineral resources. People who are supposed to enforce the law are the first to violate them. None of these laws or procedures are upheld, politicians use their authority according to the hierarchy: minister, governors, president advisors, army chiefs, and the president are the ones who contribute to the misery of Congolese citizens.

THE UNTOUCHABLES

Most Congolese officials are above the laws and untouchables when it comes to illicit activities. For instance, Augustin Katumba Mwake and the actual governor of Katanga Moise Katumbi Chapwe, when a governor, a senator, minister, or president is partnered with a mining business man, that businessmen will utilize those politicians to avoid taxes and fees due to government. That is how DRC government loses billions of dollars each month for the benefit of certain cold-blooded and crooked politicians.

Let's talk about mining firms that exist in the region of Katanga in three different cities. Lubumbashi, Likasi, Kolwezi as examples of:

- Enterprise group Bazano is a limited asset company owned by Indo Pakistani guys. These guys are partnered with Augustin Katumba Mwake this company is based in Likasi, Lubumbashi and Kolwezi
- Anvil Mining here again Katumba Mwake is partner include with Katanga Governor Moise Katumbi Chapwe, and they both play the same role in these two companies

- Enterprise Virginia and MCK (Mining Company Katanga) here you have Moise Katumbi and his little sister Virginie Katumbi are both partners to this company.
- Momi (Mutanda Mining) based in Kolwezi, here comes Augustin Katumba Mwake as partner and CEO of the company
- Enterprise KCC (Kamoto Coperbed Company), a British company with Joseph Kabila, President of DRC, as partner. This company is based in Kolwezi. To me, Moise Katumbi and Joseph Kabila are birds of same feather, both are the top two billionaires in DRC, both are very detrimental to Congolese people, both have doubtful Congolese nationality, and none of them cares about the welfare of Congolese. As rich as Moise Katumbi is, Katanga Region has multitude of rotten roads. Katanga is overwhelmed by poverty despite being mining riches. Now where does millions of taxes dollars paid by the foreign mining companies go? Most of that money goes to Kabila and Katumbi's offshore accounts somewhere in Cayman or South Africa.

As I did mention in previous chapters, to protect his dictatorial regime, Mr. Joseph Kabila has given away multitude of mining to Jacob Zuma and several ANC officials. These informal business are paperless contracted strictly between Kabila and Zuma. Millions and million of dollars roll out every month from DRC to Zuma's personal account to help him take care of his five wives and God knows how many concubines—all these Al Capone style of business put enormous burdens on Congolese and just left them in dust. The Congolese resources are being uncontrollable excavated away from DRC. Take a trip down to Kasumbalesa, sit and watch how DRC minerals are being looted by foreign companies and some individuals, you will see a line trucks loaded with precious minerals en route to South Africa crossing DRC boundaries unchecked. The inhuman side of this business is most of its laborers are DRC's nationals. They are being used in new advanced ways of slavery, their housing and living conditions were never improved by these companies or by the government, and makes them vulnerable to bribes for $1000 dollars. A government mining agent would be gladly to let 100 million worth of minerals slip away.

We need to revamp or implement a new mechanism to streamline our resources, the actual DRC government is unqualified to manage our resources. I recently read somewhere that Gecamines (the state-owned mining company) was contemplating action against its partners Swiss-based Glencore XStrata and US-based free port, McMoran Copper & Gold for being treated unfairly. I will get back to that. Wasn't Gecamines previously one of the world's biggest copper producer? Producing 476,000 tonnes in 198 dramatically stopped producing in early 2000 for mismanagement and the outdated equipment and debt burden of nearly $1 billion. Now let's go back to what I promised. If the companies that treated Gecamine like a stepson deposit on a healthy ROF dollar amount in Kabila or some DRC official account, those companies have rights to treat Gecamines whichever way they want because they have bought the rights to mistreat

DRC, as I previously indicated Lebanese Paki have that right to mistreat as well. So I'm advising Gecamines to take its actions against Mr. Kabila and DRC Government no those companies.

One of the things DRC needs most desperately is leadership. It doesn't have a leader. This is a pathetic thing to say about DRC. Congolese are good people, but their leaders and their politicians are misfortune. So Gecamine, stop crying, help is on the way.

There is just some of the few national overarching we need to achieve in order to solve some of the humongous problems that cripple DRC from being economically and politically elite in the world.

Extra! Extra! South Africa and DRC agree to develop grand Inga plant on October 31, 2013 business report. The over forty-year-old grand Inga project to develop hydroelectric capacity on the Congo River took a stem forward with Mr. Jacob Zuma of South Africa and Joseph Kabila of DRC announcing the signing of treaty to jointly develop the project, which will eventually provide 40,000 megawatts of electricity, and it will cost $100 billion. The project will boost the economy growth of surrounding countries. Mr. Zuma emphasize that this will tremendously provide South African companies with further investment opportunities. Well, South Africa is so obsessed with DRC resources and taking advantage of DRC's irresponsible government to enrich South Africa. This project signing is outrageous and doesn't benefit Congolese people whatsoever. How in the world are we sharing half of our 44,000 megawatts hydroelectric with South Africa, while only 10 percent of 75 million Congolese people have electricity? South Africans have animosity, hatred, and xenophobic feelings toward Congolese, but they sure love Congo.

Congolese need to wise up and take control of their destiny. I guarantee you that the cost of this Inga project for $100 billion will generate from DRC mineral resources—you will read it more in detail in upcoming chapter. Mr. Zuma will only generate weapons to kill Congolese and South African soldiers to protect the dictatorship regime of Mr. Joseph Kabila. Just for weapons and soldiers, Mr. Zuma and South Africa will own and manage the Inga hydroelectric dam. DRC is more than capable to revive Inga phase 1 and build phase 2 and 3 on its own if only we have consciousness government.

Economist magazine Project Kinshasa population will be increased to 15 million people in decade. Mbuji Mayi will be expected to serve populations the size of Milan's with little infrastructure. The standard view of Mbuji Mayi as generators of wealth will be challenged in DRC. The elimination of the poor will be magnified by a lack of public space and by rising living cost. To become a livable city, Mbuji Mayi will need to improve public transportation. So the population increase will not only lift DRC GDP growth, but it will propel Kinshasa as economic heavyweight city. It's such a tragedy to see a city like Mbuji Mayi, a warehouse of precious stone, has not been developed at its fullest. Transportation system is non-existent due to the terrible condition of the roads, motorcycles are the prime means of transportation, sometimes it is humiliating to see a female sandwiched between two men on motorcycle, its degrading to our value and tradition to respect our mothers and sisters. But once the right and competent leaders are managing the country, this also will give opportunity to invest in construction sector and communication as well.

Is the current government capable of harnessing this opportunity to transform Kinshasa into an economic powerhouse? I don't think so. Most of DRC's politicians are not visionary, just a bunch of shoemakers, if I can get an Amen on that one. My estimation is that at least $35 billion leaves DRC through illicit flows every 6–12 months period, which has the effect of reducing tax revenue, draining foreign exchange reserves, and cancelling out investment inflows. How to create a truly great country? Of course, service delivery, health, education, the economic, and many of the other areas of government, but at the heart of the success of all those areas of national striving are great leaders with conscious.

Unfortunately, it's very common for DRC officials of every level to be corrupted, and everyone knows it. And most of them, through the practice of corruption, cling on to power and protect their select interests. Their dishonest and manipulative behavior slowly destroy the country. They use force and fear to intimidate and subjugate the people of DRC, they continue to loot country resources to feed themselves at a time when DRC's economy, and it's health are collapsing and poverty level have escalated.

SELF-AFFLICTION

Fiscal evasion, embezzlement, fiscal indiscipline, and some of the elements that contribute to our self economic destruction due to government irresponsibility and unconsciousness, all the government tax agents have created ways to divert tax money to their own pocket—all that because of poor quality of their lives and insufficient wages. Irresponsible because government doesn't have a mechanism properly set in place to collect taxes (so most of) they lack technology, they still are locked in rotary dial phone kind of government, so most of the money collected never reach their destination before they get evaporated on their ways.

It's common that you will see small tax agent everywhere in DRC, public places, market places, business places, small, medium, large enterprises crawling like cockroaches, harassing poor women in marketplaces to pay taxes, while this poor mothers have their inventory volume at about $30. These tax agent have inventive and bogus receipts that they issue once they take your money. A few hours later, another tax agent will bust into your establishment and demand that you pay taxes. If you tell him that you've already paid, that will be a wrong answer; and if you do provide him with your receipt, they will simply say that your receipt is fake, they will threaten you saying you have to dish out more money for them. Then automatically, you become their client. Every time they need money, they will stop to see you. So governments are cheated out millions of dollars through that illicit business, and that results in total fiscal evasion, and most of the time these agents face impurity owe to our poor and dysfunctional judicial system. Each and every official in DRC have consciously contributed to malfunction of the country's economic growth. This murky business is mostly vehicles used to flush DRC's economy down the drain in national level. Unless something has to drastically be done, this pathetic behavior will linger and linger.

FISCAL INDISCIPLINE

Congolese are yet to be patriotically prepared to fulfill their commitment to their country, and possible having the knowledge of paying taxes. Fiscal indiscipline occurred when population is taken advantage of by the government, when people are facing uncertain future and marginalized when the government is very insensible to create jobs, when poverty engulfed the majority of the population (except those who have access to state funds), when people have lost any audacity of hope and are being oppressed day and night. In return, they became immune to the government and let alone pay taxes. Usually, when government fails, people fail. You really need to induce the whole Congolese population in order to even reckon that notion of tax. So the government comes out as a loser in this game, completely forgets that taxes are part of productivity gains, and productivity gains makes park of economic growth. And that includes an increase in the labor force. So this reminds me of the TV series "What's Happening" no Ronald, no rerun, no rent. Same is applicable for DRC. No jobs, no food, no peace, no tax. Any more questions?

EMBEZZLEMENT

The government funds have been subject to systematic embezzlement by its officials with impurity. They are diverse ways the government's money is being methodically stolen by its members. Fictitious employees, as I mentioned in previous chapters, I believe, is one of the systems the members of the government exploit to steal where, they create names of non-existent people and put them in the government payroll. The other techniques are mostly reserved to officials who have entitlements for purchasing government needs and importations. These officials have ways to manipulate, or better yet cheat out states. For instance, the government will have a mega project to purchase a new aircraft, new buses, or new radios and television transponders. The official whose department is in charge for transactions will submit false invoices to the government. If they were to buy new buses, the negotiator will buy used ones for less, and he will pocket the remaining cash for himself. Arithmetically speaking, they will have a deal to buy new buses, let's say 100. And the price is about twenty-four, the negotiator will go for used one, which the price will be twice as less that the new one. He will then bribe the sellers for the invoices with the full price. The other technique is rock 'em sock 'em. Just break the safe and steal all the money and move out of DRC. So all these mischiefs and government sensibilities and mismanagement have created a huge explosion of poverty in DRC. No wonder the country is ranked on the bottom of all countries by UN development program. Under human development index:

Rep. Dem. of Congo Statistics. Source: Africa Report 2013

- Population   65.7 Million
- Urban Population   35%
- Life Expectancy   49
- Adult Literacy   67%
- Inflation   4.4%
- Aid Flows $254 Million
- Foreign Direct Investment $3.3 billion
- Infant Mortality   110 per 1,000 births
- Mobile Phone Penetration   28%
- Current Account AC% of GDP   12.9%
- Main Export   Cobalt

GDP Growth
2011 - 15%
2012 - 17.2%
2013 - 18.6%
2014 - 20.3%

Foolishness is repeatedly doing the same thing in exactly the same way and expecting to get different results. –Albert Einstein.

DRC needs a total revamp (or better yet implode its system in every sector, political, economical, and social). First of all, we need responsible government and unselfish one that could harness DRC's wealth to benefit its own people. We need a proven leader, a motivator, a leader who is about getting results instead of bogus rhetoric. For instance, "Kabila's five chantiers" that will never happen in this lifetime. We need a leader who gives hope and dreams for the future of his people. If you get results to your promises, people will support you. A good leader leads the people to achievement. He has to be a visionary. We haven't had that kind of leader in over 50+ years in the DRC. DRC leaders since independence have been using the wrong formula, doing the same thing over and over again, and expecting to get better results; and naturally, they end up with foolishness, poverty, oppression, famine, arbitraries, arrests, assassination, etc. In the arena of world leaders, DRC's leaders have been a disaster, not only incompetent. How could DRC be politically fixed? It needs democracy, small government, transparency, unselfish, and responsible leaders.

Democracy will bring freedom of speech, justice and equality, and accountability as well—promotion of responsible freedom. The rule of law and democracy, not just an ideal on constitution book, but in reality. Freedom of individual within the rule of law is basis of justice, fairness, nation building, and good governance. It's got to have a sense of social responsibility by respecting the rule of law, honesty, hard work and standards of ethical decency, allowing freedom of expression. It will help tremendously in our shortcoming. We have to work for the physical security and protection of its own people. How can we get responsible leaders? By election of course. We shouldn't choose our leaders because he is from your neighborhood or he goes to the same church as you, or because it's your own gender or he came from your province. No, choose a better qualified person regardless of his gender or belief. That is the right formula to build a democratic country but my assessment is, when it comes to DRC, we now live in a globalization world, and since DRC is rated on the bottom of all countries by UN development program, meaning, the country is in a state of emergency—it needs help. I will recommend those help a little bit further under its economic revamp. It needs a small and effective government, small governments will cut down government waste in two, and will make it easier for DRC to control its spending, since it doesn't have a system capable to control big government.

Fictitious Employees. We need total revamping of our political and economic way of doing things and finding new methods that could rapidly inject a stream of new successful ideas into our economy and politics. To bring back DRC in the land of living, we must first fix its economy. Why economy? Before its politics, well, when people are not hungry, their careless about who their president is being flirted with, or where the governor is about to. Remember, during Clinton and some girl named Monica, United States' economy was booming. Jobs were so easy to be found, unemployment rate was so low, you could get around trip fares from Philadelphia to Paris around $300.00 by US Air, people were happy, and interest rates were affordable. When a clown from Georgia named Newt Gingrich came with the idea to impeach Clinton for shitting where he ate "unethical," nobody really did care. Clinton survived "barrage" of political jobs, and no American gave a damn about impeachment, so economy is a cornerstone for building a successful country.

How to Cure Economic Ailment in DRC

Now, since DRC's economy is so pathetic, I only have one unprecedented solution to rectify this error. Let's hire a team of experts, regardless of their nationality and gender, to manage DRC's economy. It frequently happened in the business world, I was once blessed to be a part of an outside managerial team brought in by a businessman that his business was off the cliff, ready to take a bungee jumping without a security rope. He did not have any faith to his own management team, but somehow, he knew down deep in his heart he had great employees that were lost in the desert without leadership. The company was losing money each and every minute when the business sign said "open". My job was to come in and do the full diagnostics, detect what was wrong with the business, struggling, and come with the prescription and a remedy to revive its process.

Change was inevitable. Sometimes, we have to embrace the idea of (for our generation), so the first step was to go out and hire a very experienced team and qualified team of economist stars no matter where they come from, USA, France, England,

Belgium, Germany, etc., go through the process of interview, and hired the best group capable of doing their job. Offer them a contract of five years with incentives and bonuses according to their performances. Their responsibilities will be to diagnose, prescribe, and cure the economy, this group will be supervised by another economist guru. For instance, Christine La Garde. She likes being busy, so we might as well prefer giving her a part-time job to supervise DRC's economy from any remote location she may be at: Singapore, New York, Paris, or Tokyo. With her, an Apple laptop, while sipping courvoisier au glacon, and that will make her get busier. She has to brief the government quarterly with her team and demonstrate the progress and every project that needs to be accomplished in short and long term. After a complete presentation with Power Point, the government now has to evaluate each and every point if it satisfied, then all the parties got to meet again. Satisfaction means there is some improvement in the economic area, baking system, revenue sharing, inflation, deficit, and fiscal all those jargon terms. Now, if all these groups of highly-trained and qualified genius economists can't get the job done, let's give Donald Trump a call to tell them you're all fired, then we hire new geniuses or nerds, whichever name you prefer.

Let's talk a little about Donald Trump. When I was drafting this book three years ago in Pretoria Detention Center in 2013, neither I nor Mr. Trump had an idea that he was gonna run for president. The rest of the world started seeing in hand what I saw back then. How the outcome of his presidential bid will unveil, that I couldn't tell you, if he will lose in general elections, but one thing for sure is he is going to kick some butt. Let's continue with our book. I wouldn't mind hiring Donald Trump to be a chief negotiator for any transaction or deal or negotiations the government of DRC will make with any foreign country such as Saudi Arabia, China, Europe, France, and the US. Donald Trump is a great entrepreneur and gifted negotiator who always comes on top of any deals he makes. To me, he is a great economist by instinct. Here is the man who never went bankrupt, he just used the laws of the United States the bankruptcy laws. He'll buy a company, he will have the company, he will throw it into chapter 11 or 13, he will then negotiate with the banks, then he comes out the winner. It's called an economic brain, just business as usual, a great developer. Here is the man who once bought a massive mansion in Palm Beach, Florida out of bankruptcy for $41 Million, did little modeling (hired a couple of Mexican for less wage to do little painting, and later sold it for $100 million). Who is your daddy? He pumps his chest. The guy is phenomenal. Here is the guy who bought a property from Patricia Kluge that was listed for $100 million, Trump got it for $14.4 million—he surely knows how to negotiate. I can see him sitting in a cool office in Kinshasa on the phone trying to close a deal with the International Monetary Fund in behalf of DRC. He'll probably get the most money IMF never gave out to any country, not even the United States. I bet Trump will get 10 trillion dollars put back in DRC and come up with a way to use IMF's laws against them and have DRC pay back the loan only $100 billion.

One thing we have to be strict about Trump is we have to advise him not to go around and ask people for their birth certificate. He can also transform Kinshasa into a prime city in the world by building a couple of high rises, Trump hotels and casinos, and let him chase in DRC where he can put his prime time golf courses. For instance, Lake Tanganyika. He will give DRC the opportunity to bring in some pros like the Tiger, the Watson, the Choi that will give both DRC and Trump the chance to make money, and he can show how great of a golfer he is. But I put my money on Tiger every day and every night—the guy is a great developer. I said a better builder, money maker, he is not even a Hollywood star, but celebuzz.com stated he earned $63 million in 2012 from his books, and his show "the Apprentice" and all this is just a little something on the side as a part-time job. He is my role model on earth. When I grow up, I want to be just like him. Most banks in the United States love him, I wish they could love me too. I bet you, I wouldn't be writing this book.

Now, let's get serious, Donald. The DRC's goal is to develop fully its economic potential. This will require a sound management (which we already hired them) of public finances and respect for the autonomy of the central bank, to ensure continued macroeconomic stability. They have to make sure that the competition in key economic sectors need to become a reality. Therefore, the same management with our main man Trump, in conjunction with the DRC's government, must establish policies imperatively that will foster competition in all sectors.

The second goal of DRC is that it needs to gain economic respect on the world stage, and the second french-speaking country in the world rather than 3 percent of Junta who are above the laws to benefit from the revenue. We need to implement anti-corruption laws and train agents to monitor corruptions all across government administration. Impunity is the Achilles' heel, DRC's government, we must enforce vigorously that laws. The anti-corruption act will clean and shape DRC political system. Make sure the offenders must be prosecuted to the extent of the law. Five years maximum in prison for the first offender..

We are living in a globalization world where you don't have to be born, educated, work, pay taxes, dance, flirt, and die with the same nationality in the same country. You need to explore your options around the globe where you can prosper. Using the same principle in ten years, we can transform Kinshasa, Lubumbashi, Kisangani, Bukavu, Goma, Banoumdu, Mbandaka, Boma, and Matadi into a modern city, but first we need it's infrastructure. It needs roads and bridges, few economists would probably argue that spending on infrastructure doesn't contribute to growth. I categorically opposed that ideas when it comes to DRC. I don't think it's an absolutely a necessity be an economist to actually understand economics. We are an integral part of world economy, so here is my world view on DRC's infrastructure: building roads and bridges will propel the DRC economic growth, as we previously stated, to have a better economic development.

We must first have roads in order to stimulate other sectors to develop. We must focus on the importance of transportation. We all know that without that, no economic activities would take place. Therefor, we must first build roads in DRC to improve the welfare of our country through political and economic condition. When the transports systems are efficient, they provide economic and social opportunities and benefits that results in better and positive accessibility to various markets, employments, and educations so roads investment is a catalyst to economic growth. I's very operational, it improves time performance, reliability, and less delay to bring passengers and goods from point A to B. It also increases productivity from remote area to a large and diverse base.

TOURISM DEVELOPMENT

DRC is blessed with such a huge tourism potential, unexploited at it full capability due to incompetence of its leaders and lack of investment in that domain. It has vast forest reserve that plays a crucial role of the second largest in the world after the amazon forest with a wealth of biodiversity. Having over ten thousands plant species, various species of precious timbers, thousand birds species, and hundred more species of mammals. The core existence of some species such as Okapi, white rhino, the mountain gorilla, and bonobo are good attraction for tourism. The Congo basin is crucial to the survival of humanity. The majestic Congo River with lots of small rivers streams offerings gorgeous views, beautiful lakes, and a coast side on Atlantic Oceans with wonderful beaches of Matadi and Boma. My favorite is lake Tanganyika, the longest freshwater lake in the world and second deepest after lake Baikal in Russia. It divides between four countries DRC, Tanzania, Burundi and Zambia nicest corner to built high rises, hotels, casinos, marinas, golf courses. and different activities that can lure millions of tourist a year.

There are seven national parks of which four are classified as world heritage a must see place. Luxury landscape with breathtaking views in mountains eastern of regions, an active Nyiragongo volcano and highest Ruwenzori mountains peak, which are permanently sow capped. A lot of beautiful world wonder views to explore, that they can utilize into money-making machine by making a destination for tourism, so the country does not rely only on its minerals resources, but it will take a new breed of leadership who loves and cares about Congo and Congolese. By partnering with some foreign investors, we can develop that corner into a first class hang out spot, and maybe one day we will have an Olympic event in beautiful Tanganyika Stadium.

How to Engage Into Beneficial Negotiation with Chinese

When it comes for Chinese to invest in Africa, there is not such things as free lunch. Chinese brings their own workers, own foods, and very into themselves in order to engage into whichever project they intend to do in foreign country, and expect to be given pass when it comes to being granted mining and other licenses. They also expect a free pass with the state regulation to which country they provide services.

Yes, they do have very attractive terms in their loans, and very low rates compare to commercial markets or the World Bank. And the biggest issues that most people in Africa have been complaining is (the quality). Chinese building quality is not up to international standards, and most African countries miserably fail when they go to the negotiation table with the Chinese.

Negotiating deal is equivalent to playing poker. The Chinese know how to gamble, how to sit at the gambling table, how to hold their cards, and come out a winner. Given all that, I have come with different perspective on how to contract Chinese to invest in infrastructure in DRC. It's called

"No politician allowed negotiation." We need a business-minded person like our chief negotiator Donald Trump. A player who plays the game to win. This is what I would do if I want the Chinese to build roads that will interconnect two or three major cities of DRC "Kisangani, Lubumbashi, and Kinshasa" proposal one.

1. I will ask the Chinese to finance 100 percent of the project. The DRC state would then subsidize 30 percent out of 100 percent as a loan, and terms will be determined at bargain table.
2. This project must create jobs for the DRC nationals and Chinese as well. Meaning, labor workers would be seventy to thirty ratio, Nationals to Chinese.
3. Make sure the roads or any project meet the international standard.
4. Roads or any project realized are subject to Chinese free maintenance guarantee for five years. That is my proposal modeled from himself, Donald.

I know what you're thinking. Maybe you're saying me and my Donald Trump are the profit from their investment. After roads have been built, DRC government will give Chinese an option to invest full in transportation, buses, trains, etc. Each city will be connected by buses, managed, and operated by the Chinese. They will be responsible for maintenances on their buses. All the buses revenues will go to them, DRC government will only earn 20 percent of the revenues. This contract should last five years along the roads Chinese must build. Area plaza, bus top area, gas station, motels, the revenues will be divided 60 percent to Chinese, 40 percent for the government. All the revenues for road toll will go to the DRC's government. The DRC government has exclusive rights after five years to review the new contract, or not, the Chinese investment will be exempted taxes for five years if each and every establishment have nationals as a majority. Renewing of contract will be subject to taxes implementation of 15 percent for another five years and 5 percent increase on transportation revenues. Any other business will remain the same for five years. Another benefit package for them, Chinese will be allowed to enter DRC without a VISA (see immigration rule), and will be granted resident card, which is renewable every year. They will be free to invest in any domain of their choices. They will be allowed to build a community of their own as you usually see in big major cities such as New York, Philadelphia, Los Angeles China town.

POLITICAL WAR OR ECONOMIC WAR

War has devastated and destabilized Democratic Republic of Congo (DRC) since 1997. Millions and millions of Congolese, approximately 10 million of lives lost to this war more than World War 1 and 2 combine, and yet, the world has been insensible and indifferent to DRC. Whereas Ruanda lost 500,000 lives in Genocide. That number is still doubtful and imaginable number, it could be 40 percent less than that, and yet movie was made about the Rwandan genocide. So why the world still ignoring the fact that 10 million of Congolese died and still dying, women are being raped, and killed every day up to this moment.

Most observers would probably have hard time determining the principal cause of DRC conflicts. They would go as far as categorizing in three different raisons: political, economical, and military. This war has taken specifically in Eastern Congo where Uganda and Rwanda continues to invade DRC every day to massacre the inhabitant of that region. A lot of questions have been asked why is Rwanda, a country that is economic based mostly on subsistence agriculture, coffee, and tea are major cash crops for export, the country with no existence of infrastructure, shortage of land and water, is military capable to invade DRC and sustain decade of war against DRC. Is Rwanda a Russian doll with some invisible super power pulling strings behind the scene? This war has tremendously benefit Rwanda, and the invisible super power economically. The other question is why this war has primarily taken place in Eastern Congo? The answer is very simple. Most of DRC wealth is situated in Eastern Congo, several mining, gold, cobalt, etc. Rwanda took advantage of this conflict to loot and plunder DRC for decade. Rwanda capitalize on DRC resources to build its country, Kigali shelters have been imploded and being replaced by modern high rises and five-stars hotels. Now, is the United Nations part of this conspiracy? Do they work to build a better world? Because this conflict has been going on in heavy presence of United Nation peacekeepers.

Most of the killings took place in the UN's presence. Congolese protesters have taken to the street after massacre to demonstrate their frustration because of UN peacekeepers failing to respond for call of help from the population. So why the United Nations peacekeepers settling there indefinitely? Are they covering up something? Are they part of something? Are they working for some unknown cause? What is the principal reason to invade Congo? While some of the peacekeepers are committing atrocities, I thought the role of the UN was to help countries torn by conflict to create a condition for lasting peace. So, is DRC excluded? I understand also that the UN peacekeepers' roles are to facilitate the political process and protect civilians, but why are the Congolese civilians not being protected? Just a question I'm asking. Is the government of

Joseph Kabila hiding a big secret? Is he working for Congolese people or Rwandans? Maybe we can go back in time to the Clinton administrations and find the answer to that question. I am very convinced that Bill and Hillary would be able to breakdown all this for Congolese. You also have the South African soldier's heavy presence in Eastern Congo. On the pretext to be a part of the UN's peacekeepers' missions, but the truth is the South African soldiers are there to protect President Zuma's nephew's interest in Congo. Let's emphasize on President Zuma's nephew.

Khulubuse Zuma was award blocks one and two of oil in Eastern Congo, managed by both of his companies. Caprikat and Foxwhelp, both companies incorporated in the British Virgin Island by Khulubuse Zuma. The blocks of oil are estimated of 2 billion barrels of oil revenue have been discovered. So why would Mr. Kabila award Zuma's nephew with Congo's wealth when we have a high percentage of poverty, unemployment, and famine in Congo. Does Mr. Joseph Kabila owe Mr. Zuma and South Africa a debt of gratitude for its loyal military support to keep him in power? Kabila also indicated that the untapped DRC oil field should also benefit South Africa and its corrupt ruling party ANC (African National Congress) and Zuma family as well. Now, Mr. Khulubuse is taking money from Eastern Congo to invest in Western Congo in the Grand Inga Project. Doesn't that make the leader of Congo stupid and weak? Why would they copyright the future of Congolese's next generation for Zuma and his nephew? Why Congolese are being bullied around by bunch of dictators and criminals? Does Mr. Zuma and Kabila respect the constitution of Congo and Congolese people?

We knew that in South Africa, Zuma and his ANC will reign until or when Jesus Christ will come down—that is the trademark of any black South African member of African National Congress. DRC is a sovereign country, I wonder why is being dictated by Zuma and his family. The DRC constitution require two terms just in case Mr. Zuma and kabila do not know that. Any malicious ways to cling in power for third term is an insult to DRC constitution. Any educated leaders must respect the constitution of its country. We are living in twenty-first century where tyrants, murderers, and dictators just wanna rule. But remember that all through history, there have been tyrants and murderers, and for a time, they seem invincible. But in the end, they always fall. Always. **Mahatma Gandhi**.

So when the Democratic Republic of Congo conflicts benefits some bald head thugs and incompetent, majority of Congolese children are left fatherless and hungry. Women are being dehumanized in Eastern Congo, Congolese who lives in South Africa are being arbitrarily arrested and jailed with no reasons by south African Police every day just because they don't agree with the government of Kinshasa. They are deprived from freedom of expression, they are hunted every day, and threaten to be deported back to DRC to be assassinated by Joseph Kabila and his administration. One thing that South Africa seems to be forgetting is most of Congolese people who reside there are asylum seekers and refugee. Sending them back to DRC would result in violation of human rights. International refugee law is govern by rules and regulations, which requires protecting first the person seeking asylum from tyrants and dictators who are persecuting their own citizens.

Dictatorship persist in Africa because most dictators support and protect each other to destroy their respective country. Loot, kill, steal, and nobody holds them accountable. United Stated has been preaching democracy for decades. I remembered one of President Obama's recent speech where he denounced dictators who cling in power for many years. In same token, why United States are putting up with all those dictators such as Kabila, Sasu, Museveni do Santos and many more to stay in power, the DRC article 70 of the constitution stipulates that the president is elected for up to two five-year terms, and the article 220 prohibits amendments the number and length of presidential terms. Subsequently, Joseph Kabila is maliciously trying to twist and turn the constitution. The constitution cannot be edited or amended by a simple individual because he has weapon to kill his fellow citizen. I think it's basically time, we, children of Africa who grew up in America, France, Belgium, Germany, England, Canada, Australia, etc. We have to ask our adoptive country to help and guide us to go back to our biological country and implement their preaching, which is democracy because we are the product of democracy. We know what takes to respect a human being, to respect freedom of speech, to respect rule of law. That's the only way Africa will have a bright future and poverty, famine, injustice, and arbitrary arrests will vanish away.

The children of Africa are crying out to western for help. Either western country stand up and help Africa by getting rid of all the tyrants and dictators, or they will be a mass of migration to Europe and United States by Africans running for their lives. We have to save African continent and Africans. Furthermore, United Nation should have a strict law when it comes for African president. No African president is allowed to go overtime when his term is ended. All presidential terms should be reduced to four-year period. Any attempt to modify the constitution would be a high treason and hold sentence for minimum of ten years in jail with no parole. Maybe this would pave the road to actual and authentic democracy in Africa, so far most of them have been misusing that precious term. They sure can explain what democracy means, but they can't or refuse to practice it.

Democracy, by definition, means the government by people. That means that all the people should be able to have their say in one way or another in everything that affects their lives, and those people are represented by members of congress. In French, we call them *"Parlementaire."* The *Parlementaire* should really make all the decisions only after carefully consulting their constituents to have a broad idea about what their constituents are being challenged in everyday lives, their views, and issues that make it difficult for them to live a good and prosperous life. The congressmen must try to accommodate those issues adequately. For instance, roads, schools, housings, and utilities. Unfortunately, some of our representatives are part of dictatorship, and they work for their own interests. None of them has public phone number that a constituent can interact or report a problem, they are very noxious, they insult public, they do illegal activities, and protected by immunity status. They have better lives and drive brand new jeep, which they freely get it from the government.

The whole system is corrupt from the top to bottom. They are there only for the paychecks. They do consider the fellow citizens as second class people, and completely forgot that the same second class citizens elected them to the office. Citizens are unprotected, abused, overlooked by these representatives all across the board, especially if these parliamentary are part of majority presidential. They are untouchable and are above the laws, they abuse women and mistreat the poor and orphans, nothing honorable about them.

The future of Congo is being held by group of uncultured. No matter what adversities the Congolese people are encountering, there is light at the end of tunnel. My advice to them is keep hope alive. If the world was told that communism would be history before it actually happened, nobody would have ever believed it, but it happened. With the right and responsible leadership in democratic Republic of Congo, things will drastically change. The Kuluna system will be humanely handled instead of the current administration of Joseph Kabila with his killer chief of police and crackhead governor of Kinshasa Kimbuta ordered to assassinate over hundred young Congolese. The police shot and killed the unarmed young men and boys outside their homes and marketplaces. Nobody ever held accountable for this brutal and shocking crimes. A military magistrate who wanted to open a case against the colonel of police who led the operation of executing young Congolese was ordered to close his eyes and mind his own business. These criminals will be prosecuted certainly by next administration. There is no statute of limitation for this kind of horrible crime and some other crimes that ever took place during this vampire administration. For instance, the killing of human rights activist, Floribert Chebeya and Armand Tungulu, and the rest of unknown Congolese heroes who shed their blood by the way of assassination or poison—may God bless their souls. Congolese always remember you for your heroic actions, and some of those who have been incarcerated for so many years in prison just for denouncing dictatorship system and were deprived of their freedom of expression and human dignity. One thing for sure is when the bell will ring and comes time for Congolese to categorically say enough is enough, where all these people are going to run to? We will pick them from everywhere to bring them to justice. Some will be deported to Rwanda and Burundi wherever hole they came out of it who are our really enemies when I see our little kids starving and westerns kids enjoying playing Xbox, iPad, and smartphones, and knowing that all those gadgets have part of Congo. Without coltan or cobalt that came from Democratic Republic of Congo, it will be difficult for those toys to operate or recharge. I understand when CNN 360 anchor Anderson Cooper said that everyone in the world owns a part of DRC, but most of them do not have any idea what Congolese are going through, or how many bloodshed in order to get those coltons and cobalts from raw materials to finished product.

Most Congolese will quickly blame westerns as the cause of our economic breakdown, but i kind of demonstrated in this book the root cause of our problems. It's more internal than external, westerns just capitalizing on stupidity and weakness of our leaders. Our new and responsible leaders will work together as partners with westerns to build our country leading into near future. With the same aspiration and vision, Democratic Republic of Congo will be among the top economic power in the world, but it will take determination and hard work. It will take conscientiousness from all Congolese diaspora and our brothers and sisters who never have privilege to leave the country. Together, we will build our country better than before as it states in our national anthem. Sometimes, we just overlook that sentence, but we have got to stand up and continue to do it till our story will be told around the world and next generation, and world will change their way how they interact with Congolese on social economic and political level. Our kids will be able to freely compete in summer Olympic and be the gold medal winner in any category of events they will participate, our little girls will be invited in same table as our young boys, and there will be an equal paid all across the board for Congolese women and men. They will be able to express their own mind, justice will be equal for all Congolese, each and everyone will enjoy the fruits of democracy—not virtually, but a living reality.

DEMOCRATIZING DRC

Now, how can we reconstruct and democratize Congo Democratic Republic instead using that amazing word in vain? We have been using that term for many years, but there is absolutely nothing democratic about Congo. The ideal of democracy is having a free society in which all persons live together in perfect harmony. So here is my unprecedented suggestion: first of all, we must streamline our justice system all across the board from high court to magistrate courts. The justice system has to have full authority of its own and not be influenced by any exterior power. For instance, executive power or legislative organ all the judges, either magistrate or high court, have to be elected by their constituents of the district they respectively represent. Another word, they are vested by the power of people and not by an individual. The supreme court judges will be recommended by the sitting president, but the final decision for confirmation would be entirely congress voting responsibility because nomination brings favoritism and favoritism brings incompetence, and incompetence hinders individual to freely follow the spirit of law. All judges would be subject to terms limit. The justice system must be exclusively independent entity to really enjoy democracy.

Our law enforcement should be held to the honesty rule. What makes law enforcement professional is integrity, honesty and self-control—these are the primary criteria of an outstanding law enforcement. But it goes a little bit further, a law enforcement has to have a good communication skill, psychologically competent, physical strength, and determined commitment. DRC law enforcements, as I previously described, they are totally opposite to the norm of good cop. They are so conforms to the corruption life due to financial stability, and quality of life with the meager and inconsistent salary they receive every other month. To transform them to renew their minds, we must first ameliorate their living condition. That will mitigate a great percentage of corruption and retrain them in all aspects of a good cop.

Coexistence with civilian is one of important key because Congolese police think that civilians are their enemies, and notion of protecting population is non-existence in their mind. That is why in a big city like Kinshasa, police are always harassing civilians day and night. They will harass you simply because your shoes' heels are worn out and you ought to pay them money before they can let you circulate. And somehow if you are as just broke as them, they probably will confiscate your cell phone, your girlfriend, or your shirt, whatever they may feel like doing. This is the trends of dictatorship and incompetent government, unable to manage the country for many years, and that resulted in chaos on any branch of the government. People are fed up with the rotten system.

I was not around during colonial period, but I can bet you, the administration was well functioning in full force, our cops were disciplined and commitment to help people were part of their lives, and they were proud to be Congolese. And the same spirit of dignity and carelessness will be soon reemerging when a strong and responsible leader will take the administration. That time is nearing, and we all should be excited about it. One of the elements we have to finely retune is administration. The Congolese administration is flat out, a fail state. The result is quite obviously by the way the government entities performs bribery, is overwhelmed in all levels.

The government workers spend eight hours at work instead of eight hours of work. Workers showed up at work tardy and leave early. That culture is a huge rampart for a country development. Some only showed up in office at the end of month to collect his paycheck. We need to change that mentality and make workers responsible and accountable for their actions in order to harvest a prosperous future. Good management is imperative.

Now, we also need to help our private sectors by creating institutions, banks for a small business loan for new entrepreneurs, and whoever wants to endeavor in new business domain that will bring jobs and subsequently reduce the unemployment. We have to take the load off government. Together, we can succeed. We also need to invest in technology and innovation for our future. Importantly, we have to secure our board with our neighbor, We have nine countries as neighbors: Congo, Brazzaville, Central African Rep, Sudan, Uganda, Rwanda, Burundi, Tanzania, Zambia, and Angola.

Our borders have been a revolving door, and it has created a tremendous carnage in Eastern Congo, constant attack in southwest, and mass deportation in the west. Somehow our neighbors have taken either advantage of us or complicity with Joseph Kabila's weak government to confiscate our piece of land in southwest, or trying to carve part of our country to annex theirs in east. They have strict animosity toward Congolese for whatever reason, and this has been going on ever since the impostors came to power. Here is couple of suggestions: building an electric wall between Rwanda and Democratic Republic of Congo would be one of solution. They will not be a direct entrance and exit between region of Kivu and Rwanda. Any Rwandan citizen who plans to enter DRC, specific in Kivu area, must first enter through customs in Kinshasa to be finger printed and granted permit to enter for a determine stay if he is eligible.

Implementation of good neighborhood is vital to our border security. We must have a mechanism in place that will control and document all foreigners' entrance in DRC. Once they legally enter, they have to be welcomed if they were at home. We have to rebuild our armed forces with a new technology equipment, so they can take part in international operation to address the world's crisis and fight terrorist anywhere they locate, and make this world safe place to live and travel. Congolese want to be active members of world community and bring their contribution whenever it needed. In the same prospective, I want to emphasize my idea on some of African organizations. Are they beneficial or detrimental to DRC? After years of research and studying, I have noticed that most organizations in Africa are very detrimental to DRC. For instance, The African Union, Southern African Development Community (SADC), and *Les pays de grand lacs*. But first, let's focus on African Union Organization. It was founded back in 1963 in Addis Ababa, Ethiopia. They were to promote unity and solidarity of the African States and spur economic development. In any organization that you sign up for, there is an interest and profit in order to be member of that. What is Congo Democratic profiting from African Union since its existence? Nothing. Instead, this organization has been supporting all the Congolese dictators, and our economy has been pathetic. Has African Union helped to restore our economy? Our mothers and sisters are being raped constantly in east, and our brothers and fathers are being arbitrarily arrested and killed in Kinshasa and all over the country. Has African Union ever comes for rescue? Rwanda, Uganda and Burundi continually invading DRC, where is African Union? Instead, this organization profits from Congo democratic day and night.

I want to narrate exclusively on one of African Union chairperson, Nkosazana Dlamini-Zuma. First of all, this lady, how the heck in this world she was elected chairperson of that organization? Was she qualified to manage the AU? Did she bribe her way there? Absolutely. The presumptive candidate who was supposed to be chairman was invited in South Africa precisely in Kwazulu Natal for couple of days, and left with suitcase full of millions of American dollars. The purpose was for him to withdraw his candidacy, so Nkosazana be nominated the chairperson. This lady lacks leadership, she was very impulsive, and quick to judge. I remembered during my illegal arrest in South Africa with nineteen other

Congolese heroes. Before the trial, this lady had already and xenophobically sentenced us to death, I thought in democratic country with the justice system that works, anyone is innocent until proven guilty in court of law. So how come this lady had audacity to influence prosecutor to sentence us to life? Because she was falsely told we were planning coup d'etat against a dictator like Kabila. Remembered I stated early that the role of African Union is protect African dictators, and you have woman like that with no sense of moral running African Union, a woman who shares husband with five different wives and multitude of concubines. Is she really fit to run an organization? The future DRC government will not be a part of African Union. They have sucked Congolese blood enough. It is time to open the door to our friends and show the doors to our enemies.

How DRC is part of Southern African development community? Geographically, DRC is located in central Africa. This came during another naive dictator Laurent Kabila. He was lured to join that organization so South Africa and Zimbabwe can have control on DRC mineral resources. In return, they can supply him with guns and soldiers to kill Congolese so he can hold on power. Unfortunately, he was not bright enough. He got killed instead. We will show SADC the door. DRC will not again have relationship with an individual, but with a country diplomatically, economically, and politically.

Les pays des grand lacs, here we go again. These are countries that invaded DRC all the time. The secret plan is to carve a part of DRC and create a Tsusi land republic. Why would you be a part of an organization that is wishing ill on you because all the dictators members of that organization are origin Tsusi and they have a specific purpose. The new DRC administration will FedEx them a certified letter of resignation in a heartbeat, whereas we will be an active member of United Nations and friends to the European community, and of course, the most powerful country in the world, United States of America. Time has changed, but some people remain the same. No matter how undesirable they are, they don't give up, they keep coming back in political arena even though they had hit retirement age about twenty years ago. Their ego and selfishness kept pushing them to the edge. I call them political dinosaur. DRC has a lot of political dinosaurs. They are one of the reasons the country is still in neutral. Neutral? I meant reverse. They don't have any vision to actually build the country. They are old timer, enemy number one of democracy. I have privilege to introduce you to some of those dinosaurs.

Leon Kengo Wa Dondo, Vundawe Te Pemako, Lambert Mende Omalanga, Emile Bongel just to name few—there are so many of them. They are perfect epitome of Congolese evil.

Let's start with Leon Kengo Wa Dondo. when I was little boy, he was dignitary in Mobutu administration when Richard Nixon was still president of United States. Name me one soul who worked in Nixon administration and still working in Obama administration? During my youth, he was still there. As I grew older, he never moved an inch, he kept hanging around. Didn't he contribute to dictatorship regime of Mobutu? Isn't he participating in vampire regime of Joseph Kabila? These dinosaurs are sons of dictators and fathers of a vampire. What could they possibly bring on the table

when it comes to build a democratic and prosperous DRC?
Haven't they destroyed Congolese future enough? The new
leaders want to do away with them. Emile Bongeli, this guy is
very dangerous to Congolese public. Special envoy of Joseph
Kabila to South Africa, his role was to bribe prosecutors and
testify against James Kazongo and the other nineteen during
our trial. He took the witness stand looking like a bum, very
agitated, his eyes was color red after smoking two pounds of
marijuana couple hours before he took the stand. Then, he
was distinctively ridiculed by our lawyers. Mr. Pillay Bongeli
act will ever be classified as the highest treason in history of
Democratic Republic of Congo, so the new administration
will make sure that all those guys be benched.

ADDECO (ALLIANCE DES DEMOCRATES POUR LE DEVELOPPEMENT ECONOMIQUE DU CONGO)

The Alliance of Democrats for Economic Development of Congo is political party created during my incarceration in Pretoria, South Africa for two years on pretext that I was going to overthrow the dictatorship government of Joseph Kabila, which was a bogus accusation because I am a product of democracy, and the only way to be a leader of a country is by election, there is no other alternative. Then I was inspired to create a political party that will solve DRC problems with a strong "Project de Societe" that elaborates all of DRC illness and remedy to cure that. From justice, economic, political, and social aspect of the DRC, I was fortunate enough to discover the truth how DRC is so rich in mineral reserves and how DRC supply the world daily, but yet Congolese are poor.

Through research and reading all different kind of magazine (Economic magazine, Times magazine, and Rolling Stones magazine, etc.) that the chief of American citizen in South Africa brought it for me whenever they would come to visit me in the prison. I really thank them from the bottom of my heart. Some of the secret I exposed here, it was during interaction with some political figures who were incarcerated as well—pastors and some prison wardens that follow politic daily.

ADDECO's objective is to participate in upcoming presidential election in DRC, and be active in all forums and talks that will take place to discuss the future of Democratic Republic of Congo. Our vision is to implement a true democracy that every person will live freely where they will be equal rights, justice, and freedom of speech, restore our economy, create jobs, and have a strong relationship with foreign investors. I know a lot of Congolese diaspora who are striving everyday to see a better and prosperous DRC. Some of them have political party.

ADDECO is reaching out to you through this book. Let us unite. Together we can go back and build our country for our future generation. It is not a coincidence that all Congolese are determined to see responsible leaders. Our country has been devastated and crumbled into pieces, pillars have rotten. the enemies of Congo are mocking us, that it will be impossible for us to restore our country. But we have a calling from the almighty to go back and reconstruct our walls. Our history is similar to the Jews who were in captivity when a son of Jerusalem named Nehemiah heard that the wall of Jerusalem was broken down, and the gates thereof are burned with fire. He sat down and wept and mourned certain days and fasted and pray before God of heaven (Nehemiah 1:1,3). Nehemiah faced a lot adversities. The enemies of Israel didn't want him to rebuild the wall.

He was mocked and they tried to kill him, but at the end, you all know how the story goes.

Same thing as Congolese who are abroad. Always hearing the bad news from home, war, famine, injustice, poverty, dictatorship, assassination, rape, and imprisonment of our brothers and sisters. Once we stand up to do something, we always face adversities, we are being arrested, and tortured by the enemies of Congolese. We are being laughed at. Even our own brothers and sisters are trying to discourage us from building our torn walls, but with God, our walls will stand high and DRC will be a shining star among African countries. A destination place for the world. But first, let us use ADDECO as platform for all Congolese to fulfill our commitment to our beloved Congo Democratic. Each of us has to do his part if we the people of Congo have the same aspiration and vision. We can achieve our goals no matter how many rainy days we might encounter. There is always light at the end of the tunnel, but we have to be alert and vigilant by supporting each other the way Congolese diaspora supported us during our incarceration. Though our own relatives did abandon us, but Congolese all over the world did not lose any faith with us. They were days and nights demonstrating, denouncing, contributing for us, so we can pay our attorneys to have legal representation. That spirit of oneness is still well alive among us no matter how far we are separated from each other, either in United States, France, Belgium, Germany, England, South Africa, Canada, Australia, Switzerland, and of course, back home in DRC we all is one.

www.ingramcontent.com/pod-product-compliance
Lightning Source LLC
Chambersburg PA
CBHW021017180526
45163CB00005B/1993